energy

AND

power

THE GOLDEN
LIBRARY OF KNOWLEDGE

Factual Books for Young Readers
Illustrated throughout with
pictures in color

The Golden Library of Knowledge is a series
of books especially designed for today's gen-
eration of young people eager for interesting
factual information. The carefully researched,
scholarly texts are nevertheless simple and
easy to read. Beautiful color pictures throughout make each book a delight. The series has
been prepared with careful attention to accu-
racy, and each book has been thoroughly
checked by a recognized authority in the field.

See complete list of titles on back flap

energy
AND
power

HOW MAN USES ANIMALS, WIND, WATER,
HEAT, ELECTRICITY, CHEMISTRY, AND
ATOMS TO HELP HIM IN HIS DAILY LIVING

by L. SPRAGUE DE CAMP

Illustrated by WEIMER PURSELL *and* FRED ENG

GOLDEN PRESS  NEW YORK

Until only two centuries ago, people depended upon simple machines and muscle power to do their work, just as their ancestors had done for thousands of years.

Power and Production

Have you ever thought how differently we live today from the way our ancestors lived two hundred years ago? People in the thirteen colonies, strung out in a long narrow strip between the Allegheny Mountains and the Atlantic Ocean, farmed and traded and traveled and kept house much as their ancestors in Europe had done for a thousand years.

Today we take for granted the many ingenious inventions that make our lives more convenient and comfortable than theirs. For instance, Americans ride in automobiles, which carry them about more swiftly than the finest carriage of George Washington's day. Our homes are lighted by electricity far more brightly than candles could illuminate the richest mansion of colonial times. Radio and television bring us news that, two centuries ago, would have had to travel for weeks to reach isolated colonial villages and farms.

Today, men have learned to make use of many sources of energy and have invented many complex machines to do their work.

These devices can serve us in the way they do because man has learned to make better use of *energy*. Few modern machines, except simple ones like bicycles and pencil sharpeners, do work by the energy supplied by our muscles alone. Most of them get their energy from moving water, electric current, or from burning gasoline, oil, or coal, or from some source other than muscles outside the machine itself.

Machines do *work*. Work is done when an object is moved against resistance across a distance. The larger a machine is or the more work it can do, the more *energy* it uses. Energy is the ability to do work. *Power* is the rate of doing work. The engine of a modern automobile, for example, has as much power as 50 to 300 horses. Such an engine can move an American family, in one day, farther than a team of horses, pulling a carriage, could haul a colonial family in a week.

Beginning about two hundred years ago, a far-reaching change took place in human affairs. This change, called the Industrial Revolution, started in England and soon spread to the rest of Europe and to North America. It is still spreading to other parts of the world, affecting the lives of all nations and peoples.

The Industrial Revolution began when machinery (driven by horse,

steam, or water power) was invented to do work that had formerly been done by hand. Businessmen built factories to manufacture things that had once been made in private houses. The earliest factories wove cloth. Soon chairs, guns, clocks, brooms, books, lamps, locks, plows, and hundreds of other items were being made in the new way. Not only did machines do more of the work, but factory workers were taught to do only one operation over and over, instead of each man's making an entire clock or gun.

Eli Whitney, inventor of the cotton gin, added a distinctly American touch to mass production. In 1798 he developed a system for making separate standardized gun parts which could be assembled rapidly by an unskilled person. Parts of one gun were made exactly like those of another so that the parts were interchangable and repairs were simplified. Later, other manufacturers perfected Whitney's system. Thus articles could be made in larger quantities and sold at lower prices.

Watt's steam engine was the greatest single step in the transition from the use of muscles to the invention of machines for doing work.

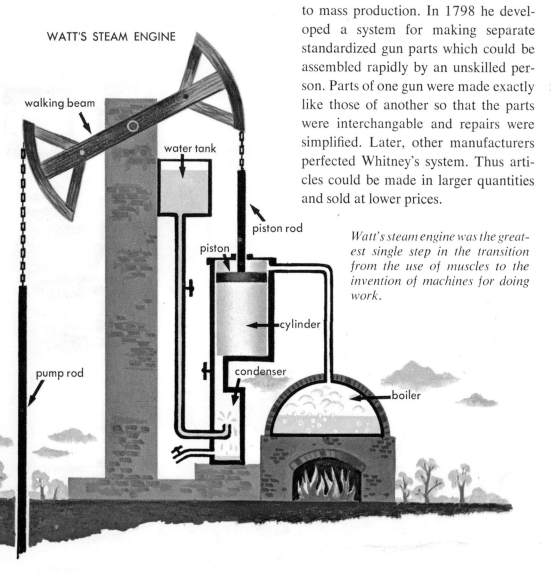

WATT'S STEAM ENGINE

walking beam

water tank

piston rod

piston

cylinder

pump rod

condenser

boiler

Force and Work

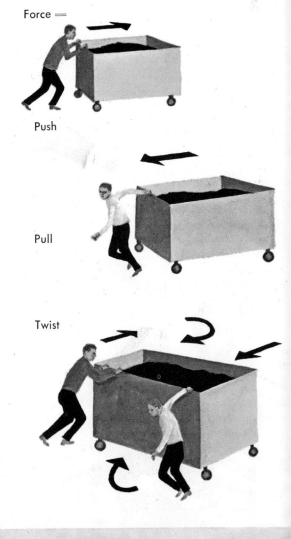

Force =

Push

Pull

Twist

To understand energy, work, and power, we must first understand *force*. A force is a push, a pull, or a twist required to make an object move, or to change the speed or direction of its motion. A twist is a turning force, a combination of a push and a pull acting together to make an object turn.

What happens when two forces act on an object at the same time but in different directions? A Dutch scientist, Simon Stevin, figured this out in the year 1586. Suppose the two forces act upon an object that is free to move, like a brick on ice. The diagram shows the strength and direction of each force by the length and direction of each arrow.

When two forces from different directions (A and B) push against the brick at the same point, the brick moves as if it were pushed by one force (C).

Below, *two forces, A and B, act against a single point. The brick moves in the direction shown by the dotted* resultant *arrow.*

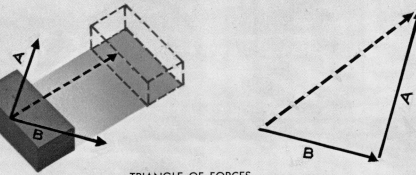

TRIANGLE OF FORCES

When two forces act on an object, each force is called a *component*. Acting together, they produce a new force called a *resultant*. If the components A and B are represented by two sides of a triangle, as in the second diagram, the brick will act as if pushed by a force (the resultant) that corresponds to the third side of the triangle. This second diagram is called *triangle of forces*.

If the two unequal forces are applied each at a different point on the object being moved, the object tends to turn unless it is kept from so doing by rails or some other means.

Rails resist forces acting in any direction other than their own. Here they permit a car to move in only two directions. If a force acts at an angle against a rail car, the force is broken down into two forces. One pushes against the rails at right angles, while the other moves the car along the rails.

Any number of forces can be added together to get the resultant, and all of them must be considered. Even though the forces are not applied to the same point of the object being moved, we can still tell how the object will move.

When a force moves an object, we say

Railroad tracks prevent a car from moving sideways when it is pushed by a force that is at an angle to the rails.

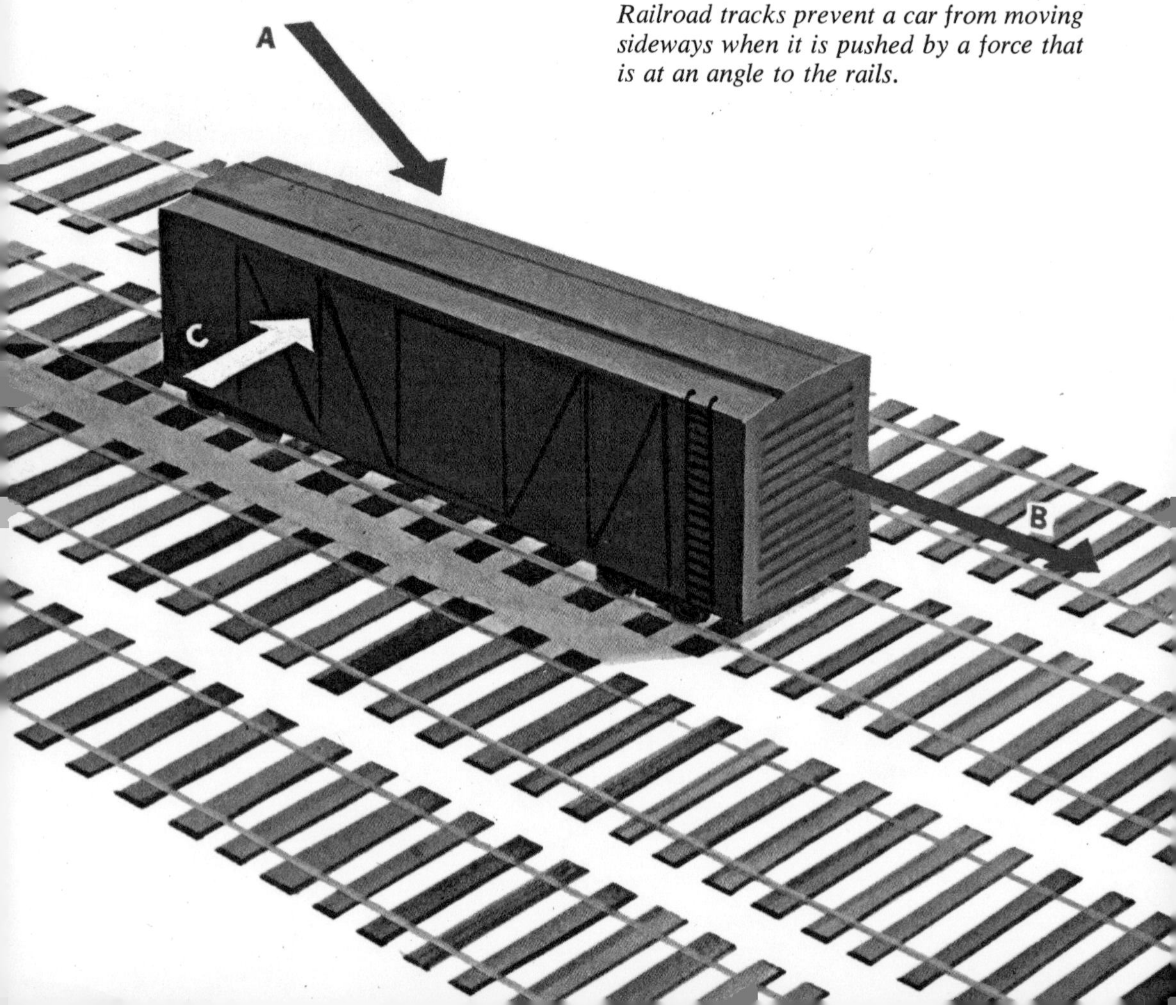

A

C

B

A lever enables a man to exert more force than he can by using his muscles alone.

that the force does *work* on the object. The amount of work is the product of the distance the object moves in the direction of the force and the amount of the force (measured in pounds or kilograms) that acts upon it.

A simple example of a force doing work occurs when you pick up a weight. If you raise a weight of one pound one foot, you have done one foot-pound of work. If you raise one pound two feet, or two pounds one foot, you have done two foot-pounds of work.

Sometimes a device enables us to apply more force to an object than we could exert by our muscles alone. One such device is the lever. Suppose you wish to raise a 200-pound boulder one foot, but you are only able to exert a force of 100 pounds. However, you must somehow raise this boulder a foot, thus doing 200 foot-pounds of work.

By means of a lever, you can exert more than the force of your unaided muscles. If the lever rests on a point (the fulcrum) so that the long end, which you hold, is twice as long as the short end,

which goes under the boulder, then the force that the short end of the lever applies to the boulder is twice that which you apply to the long end. As you push down on your end with a 100-pound force, the short end pushes up with a 200-pound force. Up goes the rock.

Does this mean that, by making your end of the lever longer, you can raise the boulder with less work? No. No matter how long the long end is, you still have to do 200 foot-pounds of work to raise the boulder one foot. If you make your end of the lever longer, you may not have to push down on it with so great a *force,* but you have to push it through a longer *distance.* So the product of force and distance remains 200 foot-pounds.

The ratio of the force you apply to the long end of the lever and the force the short end exerts upon the boulder is called *mechanical advantage,* or MA. If the second force is twice the first, we say that the MA is "two to one." Devices like wedges, jacks, pulleys, and gear wheels furnish mechanical advantage to muscles or machines.

Energy and Efficiency

Energy is the ability to do work. There are two states of energy: potential and kinetic. *Potential energy* is stored energy, such as the energy resulting from the relative position of an object, like water behind a dam. It is also stored energy that is due to the condition or chemical composition of an object, as in explosives or a coiled spring.

Kinetic energy is energy of motion. A clock spring, for instance, gathers potential energy as we wind up the clock. When the spring unwinds, kinetic energy is released.

A ten-pound weight on the edge of a table three feet high has thirty foot-pounds of potential energy as the result of its position. If you nudge the weight off the edge of the table, kinetic energy is released, and the weight can do thirty foot-pounds of work when it hits the floor. You will understand this if the weight falls on your toe.

There are also different *kinds* of energy. For example, heat energy is the energy of molecules in motion, since moving molecules can do work. A charge of gunpowder has potential *chemical* energy stored in it. When it explodes, it converts the chemical energy to mechanical energy that sends the bullet on its way. A pound of coal con-

A weight resting on a table's edge has potential, or stored, energy. If the weight fell from the table, it would release kinetic energy, or the energy of motion. There are also different kinds of energy, such as thermal energy, and chemical energy.

Until early in the 18th century, most industries depended upon human or animal power to drive the machinery. Here, horses hitched to a shaft drive an industrial pump.

tains about ten million foot-pounds of potential *chemical* energy, some of which can be converted into work when the coal is burned.

Power is the rate of doing work. To discover the power developed when work is done, we divide the amount of work performed by the length of time it requires. So, if you do one thousand foot-pounds of work in two minutes, the power you develop is five hundred foot-pounds a minute, or a bit under ⅙ horsepower.

In the late 1700s, James Watt tried to sell his steam engines to the owners of coal mines and factories. Mine pumps were then often powered by a horse hitched to a shaft connected with the pump. The mine owners wanted to know how many horses Watt's engines would replace.

Watt did an experiment with a horse and found that it could do about 33,000 foot-pounds of work per minute. Therefore, he said, let us call 33,000 foot-pounds per minute one *horsepower*.

13

Actually, only the largest and strongest horses can develop so much power for any length of time. Nevertheless, Watt sold his engines as 5, 10, or 20 horsepower, and we still use this unit to measure the rate of work being done.

During the nineteenth century, scientists learned two things about energy. One is that energy can neither be created nor destroyed. It can only be changed into another form of energy. Some people who do not know this fact think that, by some tricky arrangement, they can get more energy out of a machine than they put into it.

For example, they may allow falling water to turn a water wheel, which works a pump which (they think) will pump all the water back up above the water wheel to keep it turning. Such a machine is called a *perpetual-motion machine* because people hope it will run forever. But perpetual-motion machines have never worked and we now know they could not possibly work. Loss of energy through friction brings such a device to a stop.

A second idea about energy that is closely related to the first is that a machine cannot turn out as much energy or work as goes into it. In machines there is always rubbing or friction between moving parts, even if the machine is well lubricated. This friction converts some of the mechanical energy into heat, which is dissipated and lost. Because of frictional and other losses, the output of a machine is always less than the input. The total energy (or work) of input and output are equal, but some of the input energy is converted into a form we cannot use. The output of *useful* work may

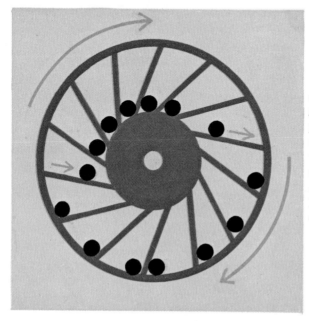

One design for a perpetual-motion machine used gravity as its moving force. Heavy balls rolling between the spokes of a wheel forced the wheel to continue to turn. However, as with all such machines, some energy would be lost due to friction, and the machine would soon stop.

Steam Locomotive

Boiler

Firebox

Piston

Diesel Engine

Old fashioned steam locomotives can turn only about 5 to 8 per cent of their fuel into useful work, while a modern Diesel engine may be 25 to 40 per cent efficient.

be half the input or less. The use of lubricants, bearings, and precision-made parts helps reduce friction, but it cannot eliminate friction altogether.

More energy is always put into an engine than we can obtain from it in useful work. Therefore, we can measure these two quantities to see how effective our engine is in relation to the amount of energy put into it. If we divide the useful work done by the amount of energy used to produce it, we get a fraction that is less than 1. This fraction (usually converted to per cent) is a measure of the efficiency of the machine.

The efficiency of steam engines ranges from about 5 to 8 per cent in old fashioned steam locomotives, and up to 38 per cent in the big high-pressure steam turbines used in electric power plants and large passenger liners. Internal-combustion engines reach 35 per cent. An automobile engine has an efficiency of about 30 per cent. A big Diesel engine may develop an efficiency of 25 to 40 per cent; 44 per cent is the record. In other words, this excellent Diesel engine turns 44 per cent of the energy of its fuel into useful work, while the major portion, 56 per cent of the energy, is lost.

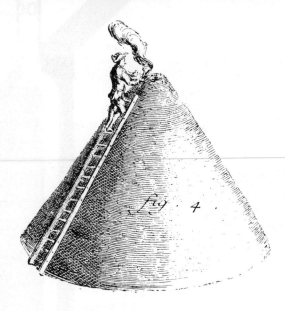

fig. 4

An 18th-century workman lights a mud-packed charcoal furnace.

Energy for Heating

Throughout history men have spent a great deal of effort turning the potential chemical energy of fuel into heat to keep themselves warm and to cook their food. As civilization developed over the past six or seven thousand years, more and more heat was needed for such purposes as heating houses, baking bricks, and smelting metals out of ores.

An 18th-century workman lights a mud-packed charcoal furnace.

For thousands of years, man's main fuel was firewood. Then people discovered that the carbon of partly burned wood gave a hotter flame than wood itself. Charcoal was manufactured on a large scale by burning tightly packed stacks of wood covered with mud or moist straw. Although a charcoal fire must be started with a fire of ordinary wood, the charcoal, once ignited, burns at a higher temperature and with much less smoke than a wood fire.

In ancient times, charcoal was used to smelt metal and to heat houses. A charcoal fire was started in a metal basin called a brazier. Rural houses in Japan are still heated in this way today.

Coal and crude oil, or petroleum, were known and occasionally used in ancient times. These two are called *fossil fuels* because they are the remains of former living things. But coal and petroleum did not become important sources of heat until the eighteenth century.

Around 100 A.D., Roman villas were heated by hot air flowing through subflooring and wall ducts.

In ancient houses in cool countries, fires were built on a stone hearth in the center of the main room. A hole in the roof created a draft, making the fire burn more effectively. It also let out the smoke, or some of it, but it let in the rain. Chimneys were used in the furnaces of smiths, brickmakers, and bakers long ago, but only in the past 700 years have private houses had chimneys.

If you burn fuel in a hearth separated from the inside of the house and let the hot air and gases pass through pipes or ducts in the walls and floors, you can heat the house in a clean manner. Moreover, you can heat the entire house by one big fire instead of by separate fires in different rooms.

Heating of this kind, called central heating, has been discovered several times over. More than 3,000 years ago, the palace of the king of Arzawa, in what is now Turkey, was heated in this manner. Then central heating was forgotten for a thousand years until a Roman businessman, Sergius Orata, invented it again.

Later, many large houses in the colder parts of the Roman Empire were heated in this way. A fire was lit in a furnace outside the house, at the base of one of the walls, and the hot gases from the fire were led through ducts in the floor and walls.

When the Roman Empire fell, central heating was again lost until the nineteenth century, when systems of central heating by hot air, steam, and hot water were developed.

With the coming of the Industrial Revolution, the need for fuel increased enormously. Therefore, men turned more and more from firewood to coal, until today the United States alone mines almost half a billion tons of coal every year.

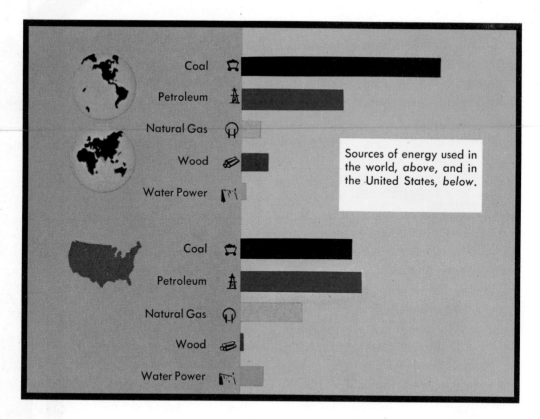

Coal

Petroleum

Natural Gas

Wood

Water Power

Coal

Petroleum

Natural Gas

Wood

Water Power

Sources of energy used in the world, *above*, and in the United States, *below*.

Coal is formed from wood and other vegetable matter that has been buried deep in the earth for millions of years. During this time it has undergone a chemical change, which slowly alters the wood into coal. Wood is mainly composed of carbon, hydrogen, and oxygen. As wood turns into coal, increasing amounts of the hydrogen and oxygen unite to form water, which is gradually lost. Some hydrogen and carbon are lost as methane or marsh gas. The older and more altered the coal becomes, the more it approaches pure carbon.

Young coal is a brown, woody, or fibrous substance called lignite, which gives out relatively little heat on burn-ing. Bituminous or soft coal has been altered more. It is black and gives off more heat than lignite does. Still more altered coal is called anthracite; it is hard and black, and difficult to ignite. It burns with a very hot flame, and little smoke is given off.

The next most important source of fuel for heating was petroleum. In 1859, Edwin Drake began pumping oil out of the ground in Pennsylvania. Chemists soon learned to separate this oil into the kerosene, gasoline, fuel oil, lubricating oil, and other substances of which it is a mixture. Natural gas, which may occur with oil deposits, is piped from the fields and is used in industry and also for household gas instead of coal gas.

The use of petroleum has risen until today it furnishes almost a third of the fuel energy consumed in the world. In the United States, more energy is now derived from petroleum than from coal.

About 150 years ago, Benjamin Thompson (later Count Rumford), a noted scientist from Connecticut who fought on the British side in the American Revolution, discovered that heat is connected with the energy of motion.

How can heat be a form of motion? The reason is that all matter is made up of about 100 different kinds of elements. The smallest particle of an element is an atom. There are atoms of gold, iron, sulfur, carbon, and so on.

When atoms join together in groups, the groups are called molecules. For instance, a molecule of water is made of one atom of oxygen and two of hydrogen. A molecule of table salt is made of one atom of the sodium and one of the chlorine. A molecule of hydrogen is made of two atoms of hydrogen.

Molecules are usually in motion. In a gas, they are far apart in proportion to their size. They move about, bouncing off one another and the walls of their container at terrific speeds.

In a liquid they are closer together but still move freely. In a solid they are more or less fixed in place, but jiggle back and forth in their limited space like a piece of chewing gum stuck to a vibrating harp string.

Thompson's experiments led to the discovery that all heat is created by the movement of molecules. The faster the molecules move, the hotter are the objects of which they are made.

In the early 1800s Benjamin Thompson proposed his theory that heat is created by the motion of molecules. He demonstrated this by rotating a corked test tube full of water between two wooden paddles. The friction between the paddles and the sides of the tube caused the water to boil.

Iron glows orange-red at 1600° F., bright yellow at 2400° F., and white hot at 2750°.

Energy for Light

When metals such as iron become very hot, they glow and give off light. At 1,000 degrees Fahrenheit, iron begins to glow a dull red. At 1,700°, the color is bright orange-red. At 2,400°, iron shines with a yellow light, and at about 2,800°, the iron is white hot.

Light is often associated with substances heated to high temperatures—often thousands of degrees. The light of a candle flame is produced by particles heated to about 2,700° Fahrenheit, and the tungsten filament of an electric light operates at about 4,800°.

As human eyes do not see very well at night, early men used fire to help them. Those who had to go beyond the range of the campfire carried a torch—a stick of pitchy wood that was set aflame at one end.

However, firelight is too dim and flickering to illuminate fine work. Therefore, Stone Age hunters invented lamps. The first lamps were little stone saucers filled with grease in which twist-ed stalks of dried moss served as wicks.

As years went by, men invented better devices for lighting. Oil lamps were made of pottery or metal with a small hole for the wick. The rushlight, a bundle of rushes with the upper end dipped in grease, was used as a torch. The link, made by soaking a piece of rope in pitch, was another device. The taper, made by dipping a string in tallow or wax, was still another.

The Etruscans in northern Italy found that by dipping a fiber into melted wax or tallow over and over, they could build up a thick, solid rod. This was the candle, which would burn much longer than a taper. The Romans borrowed this idea in the fourth century B.C. and, with the rise of the Roman Empire, the candle began to be used widely throughout the Mediterranean lands, only to give way to improved lamps.

For a long time after the development of the candle and the simple lamp, there was little change in lighting devices.

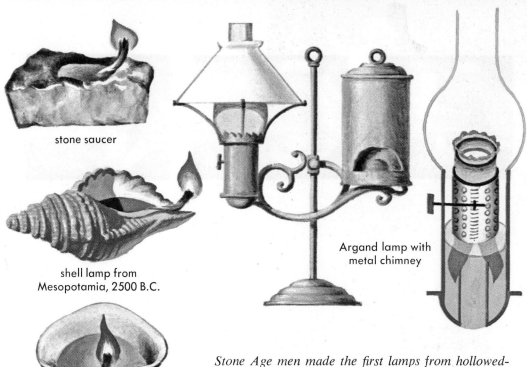

stone saucer

shell lamp from
Mesopotamia, 2500 B.C.

Argand lamp with
metal chimney

Phoenician pottery lamp

Stone Age men made the first lamps from hollowed-out stone saucers. Later, men used shells or pottery saucers filled with grease. The biggest improvement in lighting came in 1784 when Argand invented an oil lamp with a metal chimney.

Only the rich could afford much illumination at night. Most people could do little work at home after sunset. In 350 A.D., Antioch, in Syria, became the first city to have its streets lighted. Gradual improvements in the style of lamps and in the oils available for fuel were made.

Modern improvements in lighting began in 1784, when a Swiss named Argand invented a better oil lamp. This lamp had a sleeve or cylindrical wick placed between two metal tubes, one inside the other. Air to feed the flame rose through the inside of the smaller tube as well as outside the larger one. To make the flame burn even more brightly, Argand put a metal chimney above it to keep the flame from flickering and to provide a better draft.

Argand's lamps became very popular when a glass chimney was added, because this one lamp gave the illumination of many candles, so people could weave, repair their tools, read, and carry on other daytime activities comfortably at night. The best oil for these lamps was spermaceti oil, from the head of the sperm whale. The great American whaling industry grew up in the early 1800s to furnish this oil. But it practically ended later in the century after kerosene distilled from petroleum proved to be as good as spermaceti oil and considerably cheaper.

21

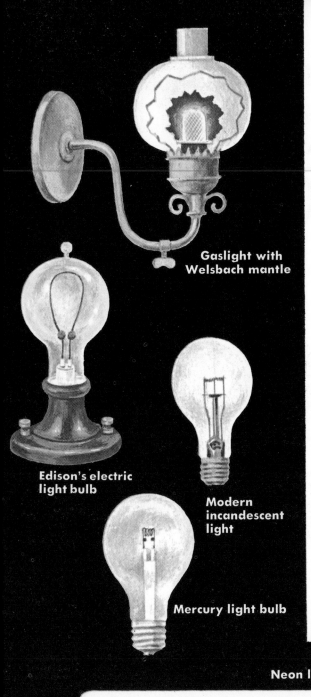

Lighting devices, from gaslight and electric bulbs to glowing fluorescent tubes.

Gaslight with Welsbach mantle

Edison's electric light bulb

Modern incandescent light

Mercury light bulb

Neon light

Fluorescent tube

When artificial gas (made by heating coal without air) came into use in England about 1800, many people burned it in flattened gas jets to light their houses. Gas lamps were improved by the Welsbach mantle, which greatly increased light output.

The most successful light source, however, is the electric light. Several inventors developed the arc light, in which the current is carried by glowing carbon vapor across a gap between the ends of two carbon rods. But the arc light was too bright for household use. Many inventors then tried to "subdivide the electric light." Thomas A. Edison won the race for a practical incandescent lamp in 1879 by sending an electric current through a sliver of carbonized bamboo in a vacuum, heating the filament almost to white heat.

Most modern electric lights work on Edison's principle, although the filament of bamboo has long since given way to a coiled tungsten wire. Besides these, we now have fluorescent tubes, neon lamps, and luminescent panels.

Energy for Living

Heat, then, is a kind of energy. Engines need fuel in order to change the chemical energy released by burning the fuel into mechanical energy to do useful work. In some ways, human beings and other animals are just as much engines as a steam or a Diesel engine. Therefore they too need fuel. We call the fuel for living bodies *food*.

Since heat is a kind of energy, an appropriate measure of heat energy has been devised. In talking about the energy obtained from food, we commonly use a unit called the Calorie, or, more accurately, the large Calorie. This is the amount of heat needed to raise 1,000 grams of water one degree centigrade.

To keep his body machine running, a human being may eat from 1,000 to 2,000 pounds of food a year. However, the mere weight of the food eaten is not the best way of measuring its use to the body when we talk about diet. Foods of different kinds provide different amounts of energy per pound and contain different amounts of the various nutrients which are essential to health. The amount of energy available varies from such fuel-rich foods as peanut oil (4,000 Calories per pound) and bacon (3,000 Calories per pound) down to cucumbers, which contain a mere 100 Calories per pound, and mushrooms, which have practically none.

The number of Calories used daily by each person also varies. Large persons burn more fuel than small ones because they have a greater body surface giving out heat. People in cold countries use more Calories than people in hot lands because they lose body heat faster to the surrounding air. And people who do hard physical work require food yielding more Calories than those who do less strenuous work. Most adults require from 2,000 to 3,500 Calories each day. A lively teen-age boy can easily put away food yielding 4,000 Calories a day. A sedentary person may require only about 15 Calories per pound of body weight daily. An athlete, lumberjack, or soldier may need 24 Calories per pound—60 per cent more.

The world has about 3,000,000,000 people, and this population is growing

CALORIE CHART

Apple, 1 large raw	100
Bacon, 5 crisp slices	100
Beefsteak, sirloin, 2″ x 1½″ x ¾″	100
Bread, white, 1 slice	75
Butter, square ¼″ thick	50
Cake, chocolate layer, 2″ slice	400
Carrots, ½ cup, cooked	30
Egg, 1 boiled	70
Lettuce, 6 leaves	18
Milk, whole fresh, 8 oz.	160
Potato, 1 cup, mashed	200
Rice, white, ¾ cup	115
Spinach, ½ cup, cooked	20
Waffle, 1	250

in food is important because no one food contains all the nutrients we need.

Most meats and other animal products give more Calories per pound than most vegetables. Therefore, to obtain 3,000 Calories a day, a man on a vegetable diet may need to eat more than one who lives on a meat diet. But the question of food is much more than a question of Calories. For optimum health, a variety of fats, proteins, vitamins, and minerals are required. These are not easily obtained in a restricted diet. The choice of energy foods—those providing a fair number of Calories per pound—often depends on what is available. Some countries use much rice and little wheat; others depend on the sea for dietary staples. Man, as a machine, requires two types of food. First, the energy foods as fuel, and secondly, the protective foods needed to maintain his bodily engine in the best condition.

by more than 45,000,000 every year. Of these, about 25 to 30 per cent get more than 2,750 Calories each day. These are the people who have all they need to eat. In fact, many eat more than they need for the work done, and so overweight is a serious problem.

Another 15 to 20 per cent of the people get 2,250 to 2,750 Calories each day. They do not have so much food as they would like, but they are not starving. They have just about enough food to get along on.

The remaining 50 to 55 per cent of the people, mostly in Asia, get less than 2,250 Calories a day. The average is probably closer to 2,000 Calories daily. These people live on a scanty diet, not sufficient to maintain health and bodily efficiency. Those who live on a low-Calorie diet also have a more limited variety of foods than those who can afford a better diet. They often lack meats and other protein foods. Variety

Active people in cold countries have the largest caloric requirements.

24

The Egyptians built enormous stone structures, using only muscle power and simple tools.

Muscle Power

For hundreds of centuries, men had no way to do work besides their own muscles. Now, man is not impressive as a work animal. A strong man can develop only about one-tenth to one-fifth of a horsepower. Compared to that, a lawnmower engine develops one to five horsepower; an automobile engine, 50 to 300 horsepower.

Nevertheless, a group of men, well organized and led, can accomplish astonishing tasks by muscles alone. Between 4,000 and 5,000 years ago, the kings of Egypt drafted the peasants to build enormous royal tombs in the form of gigantic pyramids. The biggest pyramid, that of King Khufu, was as tall as a 48-story building and was made of limestone blocks weighing about two and a half tons each. The Egyptians cut these stones with copper saws and chisels, then hauled them on sleds up long sloping ramps and levered them into place with crowbars. To build other structures, they moved, by manpower alone, stones weighing up to 200 tons.

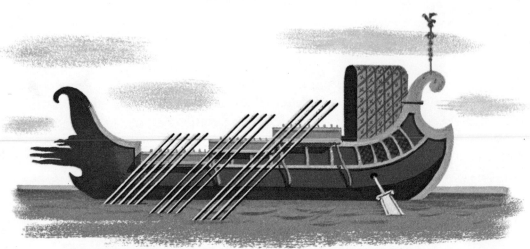

Galleys driven by many oarsmen were still used up to the 16th century.

Thousands of miles away, the Chinese, in the third century B.C., built the 1,500-mile Great Wall. Until modern times this wall surpassed all other works of man in total weight of material used.

Ancient ships also moved by muscle power—by rowing. Merchant ships were tubby sailing vessels with one big square sail and a few oars for emergencies. Warships were long, low, lean rowing craft called *galleys*. A galley had a small mast and sail which, however, were not used in battle.

At first there was but one rower to each oar and some 50 oars to a galley. About 700 B.C., shipbuilders increased their oar power by stacking the rowers in two and then in three banks, one above the other.

To get still more power, the shipwrights then went back to one or two banks of oars on each side, but set several men—eight or ten on the largest ships—to pulling each oar. Galleys were still used until about 1600.

26

Muscle power also accomplished thousands of everyday tasks now done by machinery. For instance, in ancient times bread was an important food. To make bread, wheat grain must be ground into flour. At first the grain was ground between two flat stones, one of which was pushed back and forth over the other. With such a mill, one person could grind each day only enough grain to make bread for eight people.

About 1000 B.C. or later the quern was invented. This was a circular mill whose upper millstone turned round and

The quern was made of two heavy stones between which wheat was ground.

round. With a quern, the worker could grind a bushel of wheat a day—about twelve times as much as before. In Greek and Roman times, water power and donkey power were added to human muscle power for flour milling.

About 7,000 years ago, in the Middle East, men learned to raise crops and to tame the wild sheep, goat, pig, and ox. The wild ass was also domesticated in Africa. The ox, at first kept merely to be eaten, was soon put to work pulling a plow, while the ass carried traders' goods from town to town. The use of animals to drag or carry loads developed rapidly.

It is easier to pull a load on rollers than to carry or drag it. But men had to pick up each roller and hurry forward to reset it under the front of the load. Somehow, the roller evolved into the wheel. The wheel, which came into use 3,000 years before the birth of Christ, greatly increased the energy available to men by reducing the friction that had to be overcome in moving a load.

About 4,000 years ago, tribesmen living on the plains of eastern Europe tamed the horse. The wild horses that roamed the prairies from Germany to Central Asia were small beasts. They were probably used first for pulling chariots rather than for riding. The horse-tamers set out in their chariots to conquer their neighbors, and then their neighbors' neighbors, until they and their descendants had spread all the way across Europe from Spain to India.

Later, the Persians bred horses until they were as large as a modern riding horse and could carry a man and his armor. However, they never got full use from their horses. Lacking stirrups, the rider was always in danger of falling off. Nor could horses pull heavy loads in those days because proper horse collars had not yet been invented. The poor beasts were harnessed by a strap around their necks. When they pulled hard, the strap pressed against their windpipes and they choked themselves.

In the days of the Roman Empire, the stirrup was developed to make the rider more secure. Then came the horse collar, which put the strain on the horse's shoulders instead of on its neck and enabled the horse to pull four times as heavy a load as before.

Throughout the centuries, the horse was one of the world's main sources of energy. Not only did horses provide the power for early factories; but also, in the 1700s and 1800s, many small ferries were powered by horses turning a treadmill. British mines used horse treadles to pump out water until the advent of the steam engine in the 1700s.

By the nineteenth century, engines driven by steam had taken over many of the horse's age-old tasks. Gasoline engines were widely used after 1910. In the United States this process has become almost complete. We still have a great many horses, but now they are used almost entirely for pleasure—for riding and racing.

Energy of Moving Air

The energy of moving air was first put to work about 5,000 years ago. It was probably the Sumerians who built the first sailboats. These were tubby river craft with a single mast in the middle. From this mast hung one large rectangular sail. For about 3,000 years, this single sail was used on all ships.

Around the beginning of the Christian era, several improvements in sailing rig appeared. Some ships were built with a small foremast and a foresail. Some very large ships were equipped with two or three full-sized masts.

The biggest advance of this time, however, was the fore-and-aft sail. In a square sail, the spar or crossbar from which the sail hangs is normally mounted at a right angle to the ship's keel. In a fore-and-aft sail, the spars that hold the sail are normally lined up lengthwise to the ship.

A sailing ship does not have to sail in exactly the direction of the wind. By setting the sail at an angle, the ship can move at a right angle to the wind. When the wind strikes the sail at this angle, the force of the wind against the sail is not fully used as some of the wind bounces off. The keel of the ship keeps the ship from sliding sidewise in water. So the ship, steered by the rudder, can be held to a course at right angles to the wind. By setting the sail more nearly parallel to the keel, one can

sail into the wind—not directly against it, but at an angle to it. Ancient ships with a single square sail could sail into the wind only to a small extent or not at all. Therefore, a sailing ship usually sat in port until the wind blew the way its captain wished to go.

With the invention of fore-and-aft sails about 2,000 years ago, a ship could sail much closer into the wind. A ship's captain who wanted to go in a direction directly opposite to the wind could do so by sailing a zigzag course. This is called *tacking*.

Further improvements in ships, such as using several small sails in place of one big sail on each mast, combining square sails with fore-and-aft sails, placing the rudder in the center of the stern, and steering by the magnetic compass, appeared in the Middle Ages. These improvements made possible the great voyages of exploration that began with Columbus. The master of a ship so equipped could sail in any direction as long as there was any wind at all; and, with the compass, he did not need to fear getting lost if the ship was out of sight of land or if storms prevented him from steering by the sun or the stars.

Sailing ships continued to improve down to the end of the nineteenth century. The fastest sailing vessels ever built were the famous clipper ships. These, however, were put out of busi-

Persian windmill   European windmill   Greek windmill

ness by the steamers. Steamships could go ahead on a fixed schedule regardless of the winds. Now sailing vessels are used almost entirely as pleasure craft.

Wind is also used for running simple machinery to pump water or to grind wheat. The first windmills were built in Iran over a thousand years ago. These Persian windmills work like a revolving door with a vertical shaft. A partial wall of brick was built around one side to keep the wind away yet allowing it to whistle through from the other direction. These windmills are used where the wind blows with terrific force in one direction for months at a time.

However, such windmills are not practical in Europe, where the wind blows from several directions. Therefore, Europeans set up windmills with vanes that turned a horizontal shaft, while the mill itself rotated to face the wind. Mills 20 or 30 feet high are too large for the whole mill to turn. Therefore, large windmills were stationary buildings with a revolving turret on top, carrying the vanes. A big medieval windmill could do the work of 3 water

wheels, or 25 horses, or 300 men.

Some of these old windmills are still used in countries like Spain and Greece. Thousands of smaller windmills of a more modern type, mounted on slender steel towers, are employed in the United States and Europe to pump water and to charge radio batteries.

Large windmills have even been built to generate electricity. However, while the wind is free, the windmill is costly. Moreover, the windmill delivers power only when the wind blows, and an electric power system needs a more reliable source of energy. So, while windmills are used to help generate electric energy in isolated windy lands, they will not take the place of the other kinds of power for electric generators.

Modern windmills pump water and charge batteries in many rural areas of the U.S.

Modern American windmill

Energy from Moving Water

One of the weariest tasks of early farmers in arid countries was that of raising water into irrigation ditches. Some farmer, tired of hauling endless buckets up from the river, hung a bucket from the end of a long boom that could be raised and lowered. This device, called a *swape,* is still used in the Middle East.

Another inventor attached a number of jars or buckets to the rim of a large wheel that was placed on the edge of a stream or river. As the wheel turned with the moving water, the containers filled with water as they dropped into the stream, and then emptied the water into a trough at the top of the wheel. Other wheel-shaped and drum-shaped devices enclose a continuous spiral partition. As they turn, the water, trapped in the spiral, moves up as it goes round and round until it pours out into the irrigation system.

At first, such devices were turned by hand or by animal power, as many still are. Where a stream had a lively current, however, someone found that a circle of paddles around the rim of the wheel provided the power needed to turn the wheel, and the buckets were lifted without the labor of muscles. Once started, such a water wheel would run until it wore out.

Shortly before the Christian era, the water wheel was set to turning millstones to grind flour. During the next few centuries, such grain mills became common in Europe.

There were several kinds of water wheels. In the undershot wheel, the oldest type, the shaft was horizontal and the paddles on the wheel dipped into the stream as it flowed under them.

The overshot wheel, in which water poured into the buckets at the top of their travel and ran out again at the bottom as the buckets tilted, was more efficient. But it could be used only where a fall of water was as high as the wheel.

Undershot water wheel

Overshot water wheel

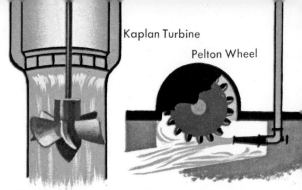

Kaplan Turbine

Pelton Wheel

The horizontal wheel, on the other hand, turned a vertical shaft that passed through the lower stone of the grain mill and turned the upper millstone. Water squirted against the paddles from a trough or nozzle and turned the wheel.

During the Middle Ages in Europe, water wheels were put to many uses. They provided the power for sawmills, grist mills, hammer mills, and so on. Windmills and water wheels greatly increased the energy available to men.

Water power took a leap forward in the 1820s, when a young French engineer named Benoit Fourneyron developed the first practical turbine. Water flowed downwards along the shaft, then passed out, away from the shaft, through a set of fixed vanes or blades that guided it against a set of revolving blades connected to the shaft. As the water was confined inside the turbine housing, it could not pass the vanes without paying its toll of energy. Hence the turbine proved more efficient than the earlier water wheels.

Since then, water turbines have been built in many shapes and sizes. One common type is the Francis turbine, in which water flows inward towards the shaft. Another is the Kaplan turbine, in which the water flows parallel to the shaft, and the rotor—the turning part— looks like a big ship's propeller. The Kaplan turbine is used where the vol-

Turbines make more efficient use of available water power than water wheels can do.

ume of water is variable, since the blades can be adjusted to the water flow.

Water turbines did not come into their own until the development of electrical power systems in the 1880s. Once electric generators had been perfected, engineers dammed rivers to increase the fall of water and installed turbines, which turned the generators. The generators sent electric current through wires for hundreds of miles to the cities. Such a combination of turbines and generators is called a *hydroelectric system*.

One of these engineers, Lester Pelton, devised a hydroelectric system in 1880 to run mining machinery in Nevada. To turn the generator, Pelton invented a new kind of water wheel with a double circle of curved buckets around its rim. Water is squirted into these buckets from a nozzle. This wheel is often used where the volume of water is small but the pressure is high.

Today, about 20 per cent of all the electric power generated in the United States comes from water power.

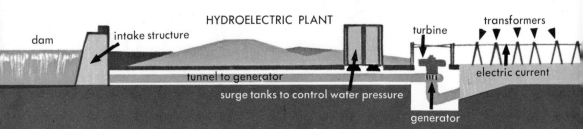

HYDROELECTRIC PLANT

dam — intake structure — tunnel to generator — surge tanks to control water pressure — turbine — transformers — electric current — generator

Chemical Energy

Matter often undergoes changes. When atoms or molecules join together to make larger molecules, or when molecules break up into smaller molecules or separate atoms, we call these changes *chemical reactions*. Chemical reactions usually take in or give out energy in the form of heat.

One of the commonest chemical reactions is burning or rapid oxidation. In burning, the oxygen of the air unites with atoms of the fuel to make new chemical compounds. When carbon burns it unites with oxygen to make a gas—carbon dioxide—and heat. When hydrogen burns it unites with oxygen to form water, and even more heat is liberated. Primitive men learned that fires would burn brighter and give out more heat when more fuel was added or when fanning or blowing increased the flow of air or oxygen. However, other chemical ways to increase burning were not discovered until fairly recent times.

About 800 years ago, Chinese experimenters found that charcoal, sulfur, and some chemicals rich in oxygen, ground up fine and mixed in the right proportions, burned vigorously. If the mixture were pressed into a confined space and set afire, it blew up with a bang, for an explosion is nothing more than very rapid burning. Thus was gunpowder invented.

Arabian scientists soon brought knowledge of gunpowder to medieval Europe. In the early 1300s, a German—Berthold the Black—is said to have found that a deadly weapon could be made of a tube closed at one end, filled with a charge of gunpowder, and capped with a ball or a missile. When the powder was lighted through a small hole in the barrel, the explosion hurled the missile out of the tube towards the enemy.

This new device, called a gun, has been steadily improved ever since. The First World War saw guns that shot 75 miles; the Second World War gave birth to a gun that hurled an eight-ton shell.

The first hand guns looked like small cannon mounted on the end of a long shaft. Gunpowder packed in the barrel provided the explosive charge.

In 1846, the German chemist Schönbein was treating cotton with nitric and sulfuric acid to see what would happen. He left the piece of treated cotton on a stove to dry and went to dinner. While he was absent, the acid-soaked cotton exploded from the heat of the stove, and blew up his laboratory; he had discovered cellulose nitrate, or guncotton. This was the first of a whole series of explosives made by treating various organic substances with nitric acid. Most modern explosives belong to this class of nitrogen explosives.

One, for instance, is nitroglycerine, an oily liquid which explodes with eight times the force of gunpowder. Nitroglycerine by itself is so sensitive that the slightest shock sets it off. The Swedish chemist and inventor Alfred Nobel tried to find a safer mixture after a series of explosions occurred, in which his brother and several others were killed. In 1866 Nobel found that nitroglycerine mixed with fuller's earth made a much safer mixture. He called the new substance *dynamite.*

Unlike gunpowder, which burns steadily though swiftly and so gives the projectile a push, the nitrogen explosives break down all at once, releasing a great deal of energy very suddenly. Therefore, most nitrogen explosives cannot be used in guns, because the bullet or shell does not have time to leave the barrel and would burst the gun.

In 1865, a German scientist named J. E. F. Schultze learned how to mix gelatinized cellulose with certain other ingredients, primarily nitrates. In this mixture the explosion is slowed down and can be used in guns. Twenty years later, two American inventors, the Maxim brothers, obtained similar results by mixing nitrogen explosives with petroleum jelly and sawdust. Such mixtures are called smokeless powder because they give out much less smoke than true gunpowder.

Controlled burning of almost explosive force is used to propel another device which is nearly as old as gunpowder itself. This is the rocket, probably invented around 1300 by the Chinese, who used them against the Mongol invaders. Attaching rockets to their arrows, the Chinese were able to send these flaming torches much farther than an arrow alone could be sent by their bowmen.

Although the rocket, like a gun, is open at one end, the rocket contains the burning charge that moves with it.

Inside the rocket is a hollow space called the *combustion chamber,* where burning takes place. The combustion chamber is open at the rear, so that the gases from the very rapid oxidation can escape. On ignition, the rocket powder burns with explosive force, and the gas from the explosion pushes equally in all directions in the combustion chamber. But the opening at one end of the rocket creates a difference in pressure in the combustion chamber, causing a reaction in the opposite direction from the

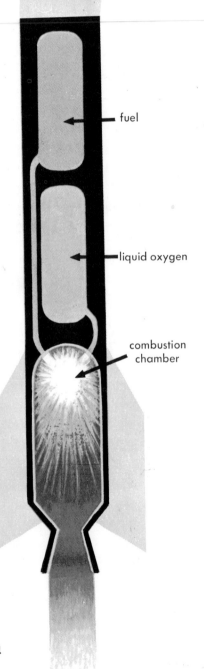

PARTS OF A ROCKET

Instrument Cone ▶

fuel

liquid oxygen

combustion chamber

Rockets are propelled by the pressure of exploding gases against the inside of the combustion chamber. The stream of gas escaping out the open end of the chamber causes unequal pressure on the inside of the combustion chamber, which, being strongest in the opposite direction from the exhaust, sends the rocket forward.

gases rushing out the rear. The stream of escaping gas pushes, not against the outside air, but against the sides of the combustion chamber *inside* the rocket. The *reaction* sends the rocket moving away from the exhaust. In space, where there is no air to offer resistance, a rocket flies much faster than in the atmosphere close to earth.

In recent years there has been a great revival of rockets as weapons, partly taking the place of guns. They have also been used to drive experimental airplanes faster and higher than ordinary aircraft. And, finally, they have been used to explore outer space—to send loads of instruments flying to the moon and the sun, and men spinning around the earth. Many rockets, such as the Atlas, Titan, and Thor, do not use simple gunpowder as fuel. They burn liquid fuels like alcohol or kerosene, which combine with LOX or liquid oxygen in powerful rocket motors. Giant solid-fuel rockets, vaguely similar to skyrockets, are also used, but with new slow-burning solid fuels. These solid-fuel rockets are simpler than liquid-fuel rockets. By means of rockets, men may, before many years, reach the other planets of our solar system.

Power from Coal

Chemical energy is also derived from the burning of fuels such as coal and oil. Coal was known to the ancients, who sometimes burned it when they could gather it from the surface of the earth. In the Middle Ages, Europeans and Chinese began mining the deeper beds of coal and burning it, at first in blacksmiths' forges.

By the 1600s, some coal mines in England had been dug so deep that water seeped in and flooded them. To get rid of the water, several Englishmen invented steam vacuum pumps, which were run by engines in which some of the mined coal was burned.

One of these early vacuum pumps was built in 1705 by Thomas Newcomen and improved in 1712. This engine had a cylinder with a piston sliding up and down inside it. When the piston was at the top of the cylinder, the cylinder was filled with steam from a boiler. A jet of cold water, squirted into the cylinder, condensed the steam back into water, and the lower pressure created by the condensation enabled the air pressure to force the piston back down to the bottom of the cylinder. The piston was attached to a hinged beam, which worked the mine pump.

In 1765, James Watt made a great improvement in Newcomen's engine. Watt led the steam out of the cylinder into a separate chamber called a *con-*

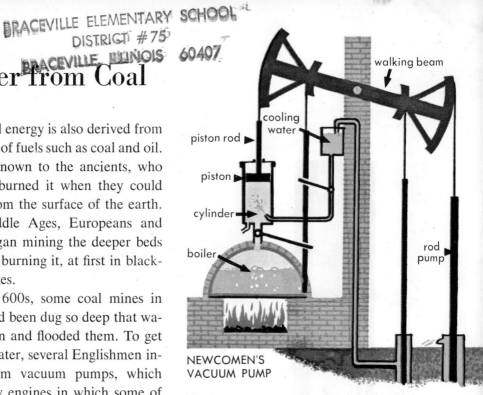

NEWCOMEN'S VACUUM PUMP

Newcomen's engine, invented in the 18th century, pumped water out of coal mines.

denser, where it was cooled and turned back into water. As the cylinder did not have to be heated and cooled between strokes of the piston, Watt's engine got three times as much power out of a ton of coal as Newcomen's.

Watt and others quickly improved the steam engine, as the new device was called. The engine they developed is called a *reciprocating* steam engine. Reciprocating means "moving back and forth," as the piston does in the cylinder. The piston moves a rod that slides in and out through a steam-tight hole in one end of the cylinder. The piston rod is joined to a connecting rod which turns the crankshaft, changing back-and-forth motion to a rotary motion.

35

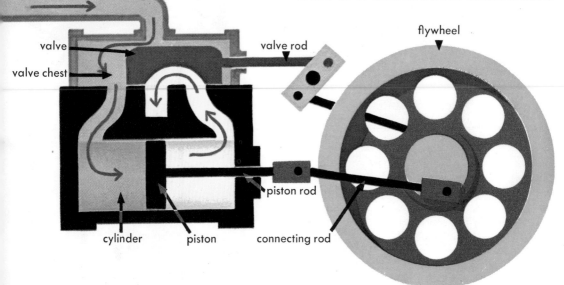

valve

valve chest

valve rod

flywheel

piston rod

cylinder   piston   connecting rod

Levers attached to the crankshaft open and close valves in the cylinder. These valves let steam into the cylinder first on one side of the piston and then on the other. Thus the steam pushes the piston back and forth. The valves also let the used exhaust steam out of the cylinder when it has done its work.

It was the problem of pumping water from coal mines that led to the invention and the development of the steam engine in the early 1700s. But once the steam engine was perfected, it in turn increased the demand for coal. By 1750 steam engines had become popular enough to have affected the entire industrial pattern of English life. This was the beginning of the Industrial Revolution.

Inventors tried reciprocating steam engines on vehicles of all kinds. Steam-driven wagons and carriages did not prove practical because their engines were too heavy and bulky and were soon shaken apart by the rough roads of the time. Moreover, in England they were forced out of business by the stagecoach companies who feared that their horse-drawn coaches would become obsolete.

However, the steam engine proved a great success in driving ships and railroad locomotives and in turning the wheels of factories. For a hundred years, the reciprocating steam engine ruled the industrial world, turning the energy of coal into useful work.

The importance of the steam engine in industry and commerce made the mining of coal a tremendous industry. Mines in Europe and America were pushed deeper and farther underground. New mines were opened up and the coal production doubled and redoubled.

Eventually, however, the reciprocating engine began to be supplanted by engines of newer kinds. One was the steam turbine, invented in the 1880s by the Swedish inventor Gustav de Laval and the Englishman Charles Parsons.

The steam turbine works in much the same way as the water turbine. Instead of allowing water to pass through the circle of turbine blades, the blades are spun rapidly by steam under pressure coming from nozzles placed in a circular arrangement.

While de Laval's original turbine had a single circle of blades, Parsons' turbine has a number of circles of blades mounted on the same shaft. When the steam passes through one set of moving blades, it is turned back by a set of fixed blades, which are fastened to the casing of the turbine. The fixed blades direct the steam against the blades of the second moving circle. There may be as many as fifty circles of moving blades in a single turbine.

Steam turbines soon took the place of reciprocating steam engines in ships and power plants, because they are more efficient, smoother-running, and much smaller in proportion to the amount of power developed.

In recent years, many large turbines have been powered by steam from boilers fired by fuel oil instead of by coal. With the coming of the internal-combustion engine and the demand for fuels more convenient than coal to handle, oil and oil products began to supplant coal as a fuel.

Finally, many houses, formerly heated by coal, are now heated by fuel oil and natural gas. So, while the total demand for fuel in the nation has continued to rise steeply—as it has all over the world—the mining of coal has actually declined in recent decades. Nevertheless, coal will remain one of the world's major fuels for many centuries, and its importance may rise again if the world's supply of petroleum begins to run dry. Present petroleum supplies are only expected to last about a century more, and coal supplies for a few centuries after that. We shall need to find and use power sources of new kinds in the future.

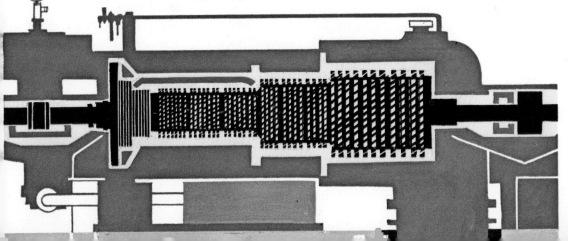

Parson's Steam Turbine: Steam under pressure enters the turbine chamber at left, spinning the circles of blades mounted on the shaft.

Energy from Oil

Men once tried to develop an engine that worked on the principle of the gun: that is, causing an explosion inside a cylinder to move a piston. Such engines were tested but never became practical.

In the 1870s, several engineers were at work on this problem, using liquid fuels and controlling the explosions by controlling the fuel mixture. These engines were called *internal-combustion* engines, because the fuel was burned inside the cylinder. In steam engines, the fuel is burned in a separate boiler, where water is changed into steam, which then passes into the cylinder to move the pistons.

The most successful of the new internal-combustion engines was invented by a German, Nikolaus Otto. In Otto's engine, gasoline or a similar liquid is used as fuel. A mixture of fuel vapor and air is exploded in the cylinder. The crankshaft takes two complete turns for each explosion in the cylinder, which pushes the piston down. The piston makes four strokes, two up and two down, with each explosion.

First the piston is pushed down, bringing into the cylinder a mixture of air and gasoline vapor. Then the piston is pushed up by the revolving crankshaft, compressing the mixture. At the end of this second stroke, an electric spark explodes the compressed mixture, and the exploding gas pushes the piston

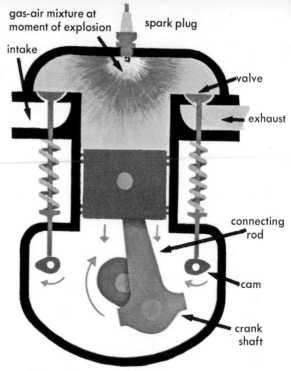

The main parts of the Otto Engine

down, making the third stroke. In this way the chemical energy of the fuel changes into heat energy and then into mechanical energy by turning the crankshaft. On the final stroke, the rising piston pushes the burned exhaust gases out of the exhaust valve.

Because the piston makes four strokes, two up and two down, to every power stroke, it is called a four-stroke-cycle engine.

Otto engines are used in automobiles and in most propellor-driven airplanes. Each engine may have one to twenty-eight cylinders. The automobile was made practical in the 1890s by the German engineers Daimler, Krebs, and Benz. The airplane was mainly an American invention, based on work by Samuel Langley, and by the Wright brothers, famous for their flight at Kitty Hawk, North Carolina, in 1903.

There are also two-stroke-cycle engines, in which every downward stroke of the piston is a power stroke. These were developed about 1878 by Clerk in Britain and Brayton in the United States. In such an engine, the explosion of the gasoline-air mixture drives the piston down, as in the Otto engine. But the next three steps—exhausting the burned gas, admitting a fresh fuel mixture, and compressing it — are all crowded into one upward stroke of the piston.

Two-stroke-cycle engines are usually lighter than Otto engines of the same power; but, because the burned gas is not so completely cleaned out of the cylinders as in Otto engines, two-stroke-cycle engines tend to use more fuel to do a given amount of work. They are most useful in small power units,

such as outboard motors and power lawn mowers, where light weight is more important than economy of fuel.

In the 1890s, another German engineer, Rudolf Diesel, invented a different internal-combustion engine. This engine uses no electric spark to ignite its fuel mixture. Instead, only air enters the cylinder on the intake stroke. On the next stroke, the piston compresses this air greatly and in so doing raises the temperature of the compressed air to almost 1000° C. Then a fine spray of fuel, usually one of the heavier oils, is forced into the cylinder through a tiny nozzle. The oil instantly burns, and the resulting explosion drives the piston down to the bottom of the cylinder.

Some Diesel engines run on the two-stroke cycle, some on the four-stroke cycle. Because of the high pressures inside the cylinders, they have to be strongly built. Hence, most are heavier

In the two-stroke-cycle engine, every downward push of the piston is a power stroke.

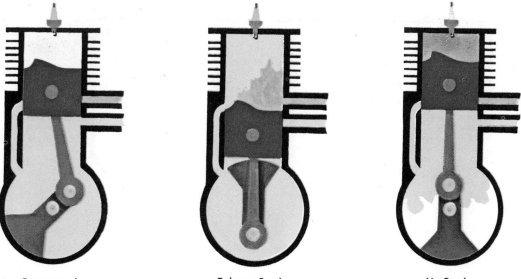

Power stroke   Exhaust Stroke   Up Stroke

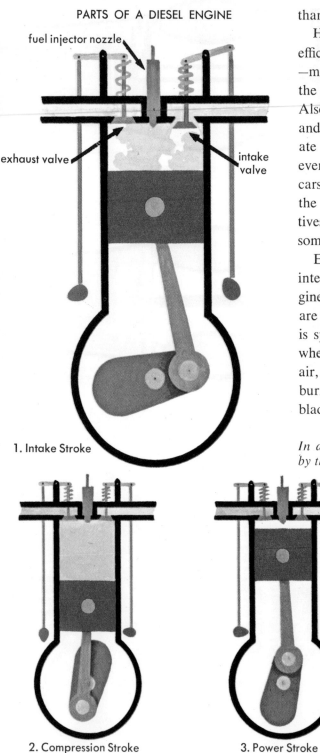

PARTS OF A DIESEL ENGINE

fuel injector nozzle

exhaust valve

intake valve

1. Intake Stroke

than Otto engines of the same power.

However, Diesel engines have a high efficiency—sometimes as much as 40%—making them very effective in turning the energy of fuel oil into useful work. Also, the fuel oil they burn is cheaper and safer than gasoline. Diesels operate large trucks successfully and have even been used in taxis and passenger cars. They have almost entirely taken the place of steam engines for locomotives. They are common on ships and in some electric power plants.

Engineers have also combined the internal-combustion principle with engines of the turbine type. Such engines are called gas turbines. In these, fuel oil is sprayed into a combustion chamber where, aided by a stream of compressed air, it burns with explosive force. The burning gases spin a set of turbine blades. Mounted on the same shaft as

In a Diesel engine, the fuel oil is ignited by the heat of highly compressed air.

2. Compression Stroke

3. Power Stroke

4. Exhaust Stroke

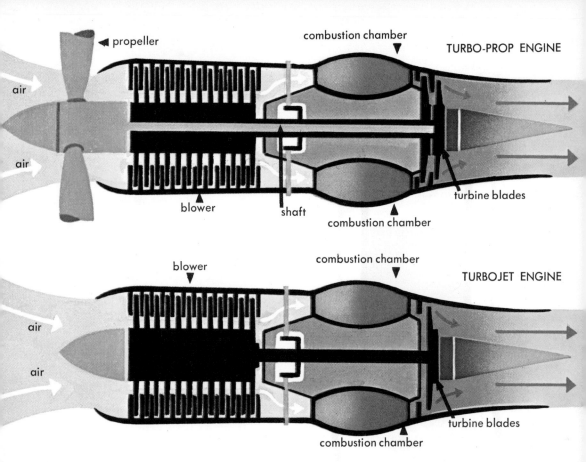

TURBO-PROP ENGINE

propeller

air

air

combustion chamber

blower shaft

combustion chamber

turbine blades

blower

combustion chamber

TURBOJET ENGINE

air

air

combustion chamber

turbine blades

the turbine is a blower, or compressor, which supplies air to burn the fuel. The surplus air is heated and expands, thus giving a greater volume of expanding gas to turn the turbine.

Gas turbines have been used mainly in airplanes, some locomotives, large trucks, and small ships. They have been used in electric power plants to drive generators, and in pumping stations. Airplane turbines are of two kinds. In the turboprop engine, part of the energy of the burning fuel is taken from the shaft to turn an airplane propeller, while the rest of the energy goes into working the blower.

In the turbojet engine, all the energy of the burning fuel is used to compress the air into the combustion chamber where fuel (kerosene) is sprayed in. The gases from the burning fuel spin the turbine wheel, which drives the blower. The turbojet drives the plane forward by the reaction between the air stream and the blades of the blower, against which the air pushes just as it does against the blades of the propeller of a propeller-driven airplane. Turbojet airplanes can now speed through the sky at over a thousand miles an hour— much faster than propeller-driven airplanes. A passenger jet that will attain speeds of 2,000 miles per hour or more is already on the planning boards.

Electric Energy and Power

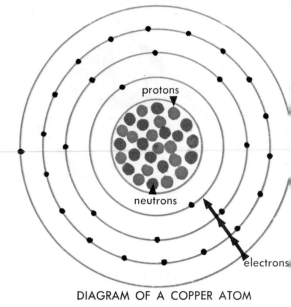

DIAGRAM OF A COPPER ATOM

An electric current is a stream of moving electrons flowing through a conductor in an electric circuit. Each atom of the conductor consists of a heavy part in the center, called the *nucleus,* and a number of much lighter particles, called *electrons*, which spin around the nucleus in fixed orbits. When a current flows, the outermost electrons are knocked loose from their orbits and move from atom to atom. Some substances like copper and silver are very good conductors—the electrons flow freely through them. Some substances like rubber are very poor conductors—practically speaking, they are non-conductors—and few if any electrons are passed along.

When an electric current flows through a wire, a magnetic field is formed around it. When the wire is bent into a coil, the magnetic field forms a magnet. If a bar of iron is thrust into the coil, the magnet is strengthened. Like other magnets, it has two poles or ends, which we call "north" and "south" poles, as we do those of the earth. North poles attract south poles of other mag-

nets but repel other south poles. A temporary magnet, created by an electric current, is called an *electromagnet*.

When a conductor, such as a coiled wire, is moved through a magnetic field —that is, the space around the poles of a magnet—an electric current flows through the wire. By combining these three factors—the magnetic field, motion, and the coiled wire, we can generate a current of electricity. An electric generator does this in an effective way. It has two sets of electromagnets. One set, called the field winding or stator, is arranged in a circle around the fixed frame of the generator. The other set, called the armature or rotor, is mounted on a shaft that is free to rotate inside the field winding.

Electromagnet with an iron core

← current flow

S   N

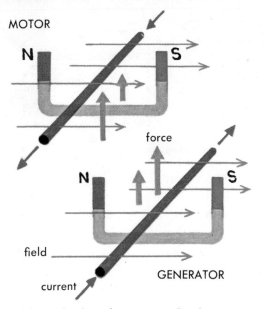

MOTOR

N   S

force

N   S

field

GENERATOR

current

Motor (top) *and generator* (bot.) *currents*

When the armature of the generator turns, an electric current flows. It is produced by the motion of the many coils of wire of the armature that cut through the magnetic field of the electromagnets of the stator. This current is sent out from the generator through transmission or power cables to places where the current is used. In this way, mechanical energy from water power or steam or an internal-combustion engine spins the armature of the generator and is turned into electrical energy.

An electric motor works exactly the opposite of a generator; it turns electrical energy into mechanical energy. Most electric motors look like generators. They have field windings and armatures. In a motor, however, the attraction and repulsion of the magnets of the field and armature make the armature spin and do useful work.

An electrical motor, therefore, gets its energy from the electric current furnished by a generator. And the generator is spun by a steam turbine or some other engine. The generator makes electric current, which flows through wires to the motor and gives it the energy it needs to perform its work.

When only a small amount of electric current is needed, as to light the bulb of a flashlight, we use another source of energy—the electric battery. An electric battery consists of metallic plates dipped into a solution of an acid or an alkali, called the electrolyte. Two plates, each of a different substance, make an electric cell; two or more connected cells make a battery.

As current flows from one plate to another in a cell, one plate dissolves away. Thus chemical energy is transformed into electrical energy.

There are many kinds of battery cells. One is the dry cell, so called because the electrolyte is mixed with an absorbing substance, such as sawdust or powdered carbon, to form a paste that won't leak out of the cell. In the usual dry cell,

Two-pole armature spins in a field-magnet.

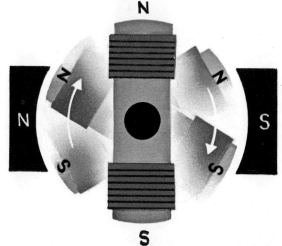

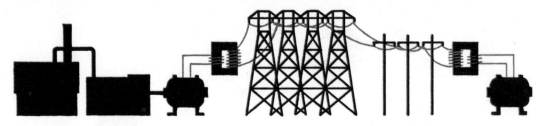

A generating station makes electric current which is carried by wires to motors.

one "plate" is the cylindrical can of zinc that surrounds the other parts of the cell. The other plate is a rod of graphite down the center.

Another kind of battery is the lead storage battery, in which half the plates are of lead and the other half of chemical lead peroxide. After most of the chemical energy in a storage battery has been changed to electrical energy, the plates can be returned to their original condition by charging the battery. A direct electric current is sent through the plates. This turns the electrical energy back into chemical energy, which is stored for future use.

The electric battery is another source of electrical energy, derived from chemical energy.

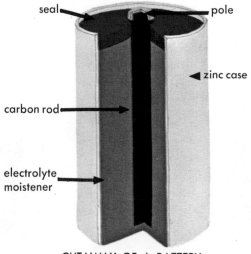

CUTAWAY OF A BATTERY

Batteries are too heavy and costly for large-scale production of energy. Therefore, where electric power is used in large amounts, generators furnish the current.

Many stretches of railroad, especially around cities where there is heavy rush-hour traffic, have been electrified. This is done by placing a third rail alongside the tracks or by hanging a copper wire over the tracks. A contact point on the locomotive collects electricity from the rail or wire, and the current is returned to the generating station through the ground.

For subway and suburban trains, each car has its own motors and its own contacts for collecting current. All the motors and brakes of the train are controlled at the same time by the motorman in the first car.

Most diesel-powered locomotives and some large ships use electric drive. The Diesel engine turns a generator, which supplies electric current to motors. These motors turn the wheels or propellers. Electric power has many advantages. It is smooth, clean, and quiet; it works well over a wide range of speeds; it avoids clashing gears; and it makes it easy to reverse the machine to run backwards.

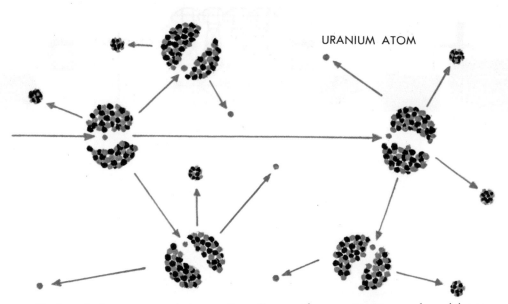

Nuclear fission causes a chain reaction. Two or three neutrons are released from each atom which in turn bombard and split other atoms, releasing more neutrons.

Nuclear Energy

Once men thought that atoms never broke or split. About 1900, however, the French scientists Pierre and Marie Curie discovered that the atoms of the heavy metal radium do split of their own accord, throwing out smaller particles and changing into new elements.

Then it was found that the nucleus, or central part of an atom, is made up of a number of particles called protons and neutrons. Each of these particles is about 1,850 times as heavy as one of the electrons that orbit around the nucleus.

The atoms of radium and several other heavy elements, called *radioactive* elements, break down from time to time, throwing out particles consisting

of protons and neutrons at one stage and electrons at another. Radium, in fact, is but one of many forms through which atoms of the metal uranium pass as they break down into lead.

During the 1930s it was discovered that the breakdown of some elements could release tremendous amounts of energy. A ton of uranium, for instance, could release about three million times as much energy during fission or splitting as a ton of coal releases while burning. The natural breakdown of uranium and radium takes place at a slow, fixed rate. But scientists found that they could vastly speed up the breakdown of some elements by shooting neutrons at the nuclei. This splitting of atoms is called

45

nuclear fission. When enough of the element is present, the fission increases of its own accord as each nucleus, breaking apart, releases additional neutrons. These split more atoms and, in turn, release more neutrons. This kind of action, which goes on at a rapidly increasing rate, is called a *chain reaction.* Therefore, if enough uranium or plutonium, an artificial radioactive element, is thrown together at once, it explodes with a terrific release of energy. That is how atomic bombs work.

Nuclear energy can also be put to peaceful uses in nuclear power plants, where the rate of fission of radioactive elements is strictly controlled. One such plant is a steam plant in which water is turned into steam by the heat given off in the fission process.

The heart of the plant is a nuclear *reactor,* which is made up of the fuel, the moderator, the control rods, the coolant, and the heat exchanger.

The *fuel* is uranium or plutonium. The metal is shaped into rods about the size of baseball bats and pushed by machinery into the inside of the reactor.

The *moderator* may be water or rods of graphite. The purpose of the moderator is to slow down the flying neutrons to speeds at which they are most effective in breaking down other atoms, thereby causing fission.

The *control rods* are made up of cadmium steel or boron carbide. Their purpose is to shut off the reaction. When pushed into the structure, these control rods absorb enough neutrons to slow down or stop fission. The fuel, moderator, and control rods are together called an *atomic pile.*

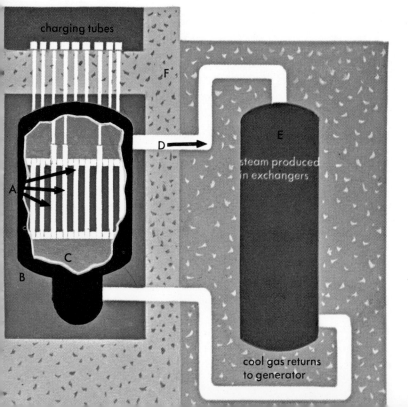

charging tubes

F

D

E

steam produced in exchangers

A

C

B

cool gas returns to generator

Atomic reactor: Uranium fuel rods (A) in the reactor (B) heat, by nuclear fission, carbon dioxide in the pressure chamber (C). The hot CO_2 is led by pipes (D) to the exchanger (E) in which water (also enclosed in tubing), is turned into steam. The steam is used to supply power to turbines, which operate generators. The reactor itself is encased in an 8-foot thick concrete shield (F).

The *coolant* is the fluid that flows through the reactor. It may be water, gas, or molten sodium metal. The coolant is heated by the pile. The hot fluid flows through pipes to a *heat exchanger,* a device like a boiler. There it gives up its heat to boil ordinary water, though it does not mix with the water. The steam from this boiling water spins a turbine, which runs an electric generator.

After the Second World War, several nations built nuclear power plants. Several dozen are now planned or in operation. The electric power generated by these plants costs more than power from coal or oil where oil or coal do not have to be shipped great distances. However, governments are aware that a new source of power is very desirable and will be more so in the future. Moreover, it is hoped that, as more nuclear power plants are built, the cost of nuclear energy will gradually drop.

Some nations have no coal, petroleum, or water power of their own. Therefore, they must sell products abroad to pay for the coal and oil they import. Such nations hope that nuclear power plants will give them an independent and efficient source of energy.

The United States and the Soviet Union have developed ships run by nuclear energy. This is useful on all kinds of large ships but especially in submarines. Older submarines are powered by Diesel engines when they run at or near the surface and use storage batteries deep under water. Since their batteries run

A nuclear power plant in England

down in about eight hours, the older submarines have to come to the surface from time to time to recharge their batteries by means of their Diesels and electric generators. Nuclear submarines can stay under water for months at a time, since they obtain their energy from sealed reactors that do not require air.

Engineers are now designing nuclear power plants for locomotives and airplanes. Here, however, the difficulties are much greater because of the weight of such plants. Nuclear fission reactors give out dangerous radiations; hence the pile must have thick walls around it. For this reason it is not likely that nuclear power will ever be used in automobiles or small boats. Experiments on nuclear fusion, which may provide great amounts of energy without radioactive wastes, are also underway.

47

Energy from Other Sources

At present, coal, petroleum, falling water, uranium, and other atomic fuels can take care of the world's demand for energy. However, the world's population is growing fast, and the demand for energy is growing even faster as more nations become industrialized. Moreover, the earth contains only so much coal, petroleum, uranium, and thorium. When these are gone, other sources of energy will be needed.

Engineers have worked on several unusual ways of getting available energy. One such idea is to use the tides. When the difference between high and low tides is great, especially in a bay with a narrow opening, one can put up a dam to trap the tidal flow. The rising tide turns turbines as it flows into the basin; the falling tide turns them as it runs out. In 1935 work was started on such a system in the Bay of Fundy between Maine and New Brunswick. Known as the Passamaquoddy Tidal Power Project, it became a political "football" and work stopped a year later. Recently, plans for this project have been revived. Meanwhile, one such plant has been built in France, and others are planned.

A French engineer, Georges Claude, developed an interesting plan for getting energy from sea water. This plan uses the difference in temperature between the water at the surface of the sea and of the water deep down. Claude built a plant including a boiler and a steam turbine, which operated under such low pressure that the water would boil at about 80° F.—the surface temperature of tropical oceans. Then he condensed this steam by means of cold water pumped up through a long pipe from the ocean depths.

Claude built two such plants, which he tested on the coasts of Cuba and Brazil in the 1930s. His low-pressure boilers operated well. But he found that there were problems of efficiency and distribution to be solved as well as plant improvement before this idea could be put into practice.

Since the sun sheds energy as light and heat in excess of man's needs, scientists have tried to use this energy directly. However, solar radiation is spread out thinly, making the collection of enough radiation from any one place a problem.

Still, some steam engines have been successfully built whose boilers are heated by sunlight, focused on the boiler tubes by mirrors. In some of the new solar furnaces, temperatures as high as 5,500 degrees have been obtained.

However, these solar power plants have not yet been able to compete with coal-fired plants. For one thing, it takes a lot of mirror—200 to 300 square feet of it—to generate one horsepower. The separate mirrors must be cleaned and protected from rust. All this makes the plant expensive.

Moreover, the sun is below the horizon half the time, and even in daytime it is often hidden by clouds. In the north temperate zone, where most of the big industries are, it is hidden more than half the daylight hours. In some parts of the world, though, small solar heaters are used to warm water for household use. At present, the new high-temperature solar furnaces may be useful for research but they are not yet practical for widespread commercial or home use.

There are also devices called photoelectric cells, which generate a small current when light falls upon them. Photoelectric cells are used to work electric instruments and to power small radios. They are about 12 per cent efficient.

Another way of using the sun's energy would be to grow plants—sugar beets, for instance—and turn this sugar into alcohol, which is an excellent fuel. In the future, however, the world's farm land will be too urgently needed for the growing of food to make this practical.

A solar power plant gathers the sun's rays on a giant mirror, which reflects them on a concave mirror (far right). *The concentrated rays are then beamed at the fuel container.*

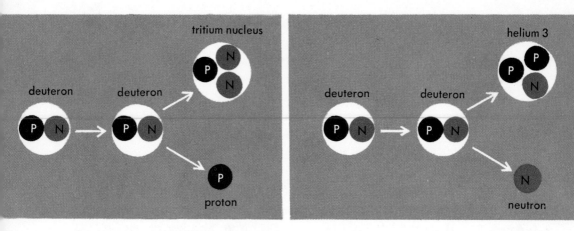

The diagram above shows two possible reactions which might occur in nuclear fusion.

A small but useful source of energy is *geothermal* energy, the energy of the earth's heat. In many parts of the earth there are volcanic areas where natural steam coming from vents can be captured and made to run turbines. In Iceland hot springs of volcanic origin have been tapped on a large scale. Most of the homes and public buildings in the capital city, Reykjavík, are now heated by hot water pumped from underground wells and piped 10 miles overland to the city. Eventually, deeper wells yielding steam will be drilled, and this steam will be used to run steam-turbine generators and produce electric current. Such a plant already generates electricity at Larderello, Italy.

The power source with the largest promise, but which also presents the greatest technical difficulties, is that of *fusion* power. Unlike atomic fission or splitting, this depends upon the nuclear reaction of joining hydrogen atoms together. If the element deuterium, a variety of hydrogen with atoms twice as heavy as those of ordinary hydrogen, can be heated to a high enough temperature, these atoms will join to form helium and release enormous energy in so doing.

The main problems are to raise deuterium to a temperature of millions of degrees and to keep it from melting its container while so heated. In 1960 the temperature of 60,000,000 degrees Fahrenheit was reached in a deuterium fusion reaction, which lasted for 1/1000 of a second.

Several governments have scientists working on fusion power. If they can overcome their difficulties, there will be enough available energy for a long time. Only one out of every 6,600 hydrogen atoms is deuterium. That may not sound like much, but there is so much hydrogen in the water of the oceans that, if the deuterium could be removed and used, it would furnish enough energy to last mankind for thousands of years.

Future Sources of Energy

Today, as far as we can estimate, about 60 per cent of the world's power comes from coal, 30 per cent from petroleum, 5 per cent from water, and smaller amounts from natural gas, uranium, wood, and other sources. In recent years, coal production has been going down slightly, while petroleum production has vastly increased. Production of hydroelectric energy has also risen steeply but is still much smaller than that of coal.

The fossil fuels—coal and petroleum—are being formed far more slowly than they are being used up. They are being consumed in large amounts and also at an ever-increasing rate.

Moreover, we use them in wasteful ways. Large American automobiles use more gasoline than they really need to get from place to place. In old British houses, where coal is burned in open fireplaces, most of the heat escapes up the chimney. The oil companies in the Near East burn off the natural gas in their oil fields because there is no local market for it.

Nobody knows for sure how long the earth's supplies of coal and petroleum will last. Up to now, geologists have been able to find new oil fields or increase the production in old fields faster than the world's rate of consumption has increased. However, this cannot go on forever, and much of the world has already been explored for petroleum.

Estimates show that the world may begin running out of petroleum by the end of this century, even though the supply can be stretched by refining petroleum from oil shale—a fine-grained sediment containing small amounts of petroleum. Of course, not all the wells will give out at once. As the supply of

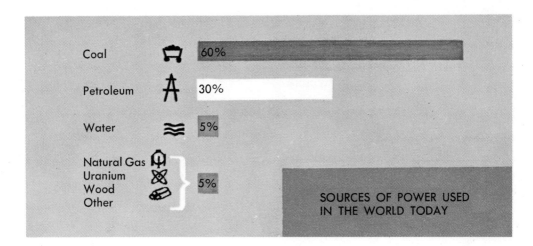

Coal		60%
Petroleum		30%
Water		5%
Natural Gas Uranium Wood Other		5%

SOURCES OF POWER USED IN THE WORLD TODAY

cheap petroleum diminishes, the price of petroleum products will rise until, some time in the next century, they may become too costly for common use.

Coal can be used to manufacture petroleum-like products by chemical processes. However, more than half the coal is consumed to furnish the energy needed to build up gasoline-like liquid compounds. So petroleum products made from coal cost several times as much as those from oil wells.

As a result, one of the big changes of the next century will probably be the end of cheap gasoline. Gasoline will no doubt continue to be produced, but it may be restricted to public vehicles. As for private automobiles, either people may have to go back to riding on trains, or somebody will have to invent an automobile that does not use gasoline.

In the early days of the automobile, electric automobiles, driven by storage batteries, were common. They were safe and easy to run, but they could not go more than a few dozen miles before the batteries ran down and had to be recharged. So they went out of use.

Today, plans for electric cars are again being considered by major automobile manufacturers. Renewed interest is due to several factors. Large cities have been fighting the problem of air pollution from gasoline-engine exhaust fumes. Quiet-running, battery-driven cars do not emit such fumes, and city planners have therefore recommended their use. Also, the recent consumer demand for smaller cars, especially as second cars for local driving, makes the short-ranged but economical electric car more marketable. Battery-driven golf carts and small delivery trucks are now widely used, and at least one experimental electric automobile has been tested. With the development of lighter, longer-lasting batteries, we can expect even greater use of electric cars.

Hydroelectric power can be increased. Water power has the great advantage that it does not give out, although individual dams may become less effective through silting. However, with the growth of the world's population, it is unlikely that, even if all the good hydroelectric sites were dammed and developed, hydroelectricity could furnish all the energy needed. It could probably supply only a small fraction—perhaps an eighth or a tenth—of the total. And nuclear energy will probably be able to make up the difference between the demand for energy and the supply of fossil fuels for a long time to come—probably for the next thousand years.

One of our best hopes for the future lies in developing ways to conserve what fuels we have. New methods of making electricity directly from fuel, without using generators, are being developed. These methods, when perfected, should help to conserve our fuels.

In fact, it looks as though the engine we shall have the most trouble keeping fueled is the human engine—ourselves. No matter how much more land we farm and how efficiently we do it, the growth of the earth's population bids fair to catch up with food production. At its present rate, the earth's population doubles about every fifty years. This means that in 100 years there will be four times as many people; in 150 years, eight times as many; and so on. In about 500 years there will be about a thousand times as many.

At this rate, in about 1,400 years there would be one human being for every two square feet of land surface on the globe. As a man needs that much space just to stand on, that would mean "standing room only" for sure.

Obviously, the earth's population could never attain any such figure. Something is bound to stop it long before it reaches that point—even if that something is starvation.

So, our descendants may run out of oil; they may run out of coal; they may run out of uranium. But we can be sure that they will never run out of problems. To solve these, they will have to use sources of energy not yet discovered or developed. But, to do this we first need power of a kind not yet discussed in this book—brain power. So the world will need scientists and engineers and education for all, so that it can master its problems and make the good life possible to all mankind.

In the past 300 years, the world's population has grown from 500,000,000 to about 3,000,000,000.

WORLD POPULATION GROWTH (IN BILLIONS)

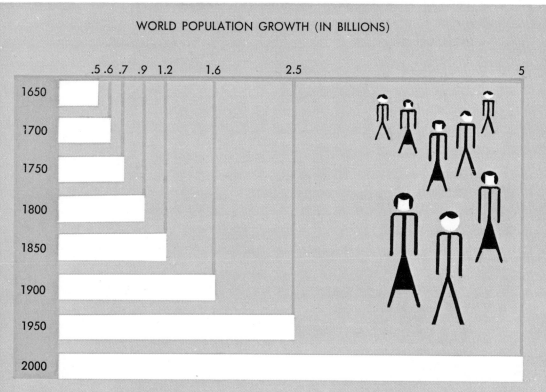

Index

PICTURE CREDITS: p. 47, British Information Service; p. 49, Russ Kinne.

GOLDEN LIBRARY OF KNOWLEDGE